the little book of
Chocolate

Penguin Books

Penguin Books Australia Ltd
487 Maroondah Highway, PO Box 257
Ringwood, Victoria 3134, Australia
Penguin Books Ltd
Harmondsworth, Middlesex, England
Viking Penguin, A Division of Penguin Books USA Inc.
375 Hudson Street, New York, New York 10014, USA
Penguin Books Canada Limited
10 Alcorn Avenue, Toronto, Ontario, Canada M4V 3B2
Penguin Books (NZ) Ltd
Cnr Rosedale and Airborne Roads, Albany, Auckland, New Zealand

First published by Penguin Books Australia 1998

3 5 7 9 10 8 6 4

Designed by Marina Messiha, Penguin Design Studio
Cover photography by Mark Chew
Illustrations by Tracie Grimwood
Typeset by Post Pre-Press Group
Printed in Australia by Australian Print Group, Maryborough, Victoria

National Library of Australia
Cataloguing-in-Publication data:

The little book of chocolate.
ISBN 0 14 027480 4.
1. Chocolate. 2. Confectionery.
641.3374

Chocolate

'Chocolate! Now that is a word that conjures up
describable ecstasies. Truffles, bonbons,
peppermint patties, lollipops, cakes, cookies, and
more. Breathes there a man, woman or child
who has not lusted after it, devoured it, and
moments later dreamed of it still?'

Elaine González, American artist

chocolate, *n.* **1.** a preparation of the seeds of cacao, roasted, husked, and ground (without removing any of the fat), often sweetened and flavoured, as with vanilla.

2. a beverage or confection made from this.
3. dark brown. **4.** a divine substance
inspiring passion in those who consume it.
[Sp., from Nahuatl *chocoatl* bitter water]

Chocolate is . . .

luscious
decadent
divine
seductive
heavenly

Chocolate

chocoholic, *n. Colloq.* **1.** someone whose constant craving for and delight in chocolate suggests addiction. **2.** a person who compulsively consumes chocolate.

Chocolate

Before 2000 BC Maya Indians discover cocoa trees growing in the rainforests of Central America.

The **word** 'chocolate' comes from the Mayan word *xocoatl*, and the word 'cocoa' from the Aztec *cacahuatl*. In Mexico the beverage was called *chocolath*, from *lath* (water) and *choco*. Supposedly the Spaniards found the Mexican word hard to pronounce and called it *cacao*.

'Never mind about 1066 William the Conqueror, 1087 William the Second. Such things are not going to affect one's life . . .

Chocolate

'But 1932 the Mars Bar and 1936 Maltesers
and 1937 the Kit Kat – these dates are
milestones in history and should be seared into
the memory of every child in the country.'

Roald Dahl, British writer

The **cocoa** (or **cacao**) **bean**, which is the main ingredient of chocolate, is the seed found in the fruit pod of a tropical tree that has been cultivated in South America for over 3000 years.

The **cacao tree** can only be found within ten degrees latitude of the Equator, grows only above 250 feet above sea level, and needs plenty of moisture, a rich soil and shade.

Chocolate tastes good with . . .

almonds
walnuts
hazelnuts
pecans
peanuts

Chocolate

The cacao tree was christened *Theobroma cacao* by the great Swedish botanist Linnaeus. This translates from the Greek as **'the food of the gods'**.

Cocoa trees start producing pods when they are three to five years old. Amazingly, out of 10,000 blossoms produced by each tree in a year, only twenty to thirty will become pods. Each pod contains approximately forty seeds, which are the **cocoa beans**.

AD 600 The cocoa tree is cultivated by the Maya in Yucatán. They use the beans as currency.

'The divine drink, which builds up resistance and fights fatigue. A cup of this precious drink permits a man to walk for a whole day without food.'

Montezuma (c.1480–1520),
Aztec emperor

Chocolate

Did you know that the traditional **Aztec chocolate drink** contained not only chocolate and water but also chilli, saffron, cinnamon, dried ginger and vanilla?

Sugar and milk were not added, so this would have been a very different chocolate experience to the one most of us know today.

It is the **roasting** of the cocoa beans that gives chocolate its distinctive flavour. During the chocolate production process, beans are roasted at approximately 121–149°C (250–300°F).

'Chocolate makes otherwise normal people melt into strange states of ecstasy.'

John West

Christopher Columbus is responsible for the introduction of the cacao bean to Europe, returning to Spain in 1492 with some beans acquired on one of his journeys to the New World.

1519 Hernando Cortez conquers the court of Emperor Montezuma of Mexico and takes chocolate back to Spain with him. There, it becomes popular in the court of Madrid. As it is heavily taxed, it is primarily a drink of the upper class.

The Spanish so successfully kept the delights of the cacao bean secret from the rest of Europe that when sea captains such as the Englishman Sir Francis Drake (1545–96) captured **Spanish galleons** on the high seas, they usually threw the bags of cacao beans overboard, thinking them worthless.

'The chief use they make of this cocoa is in a drink which they call chocolate, whereof they make great account, foolishly and without reason; for it is loathsome to such as are not acquainted with it . . .'

José Acosta, Spanish Jesuit historian, writing in 1604

Chocolat
(traditional chocolate drink)

Break about 40 g of sweet chocolate into pieces and then place the pieces with a small amount of water or hot milk in a saucepan on low heat. Cover the saucepan. Once the chocolate has softened, take it off the stove and, using either a whisk or a wooden spoon, make a smooth paste . . .

Chocolate

Add two to three tablespoons of boiling liquid (water or milk), stir, then add the rest of the liquid. Stir continuously, but do not allow this mixture to boil.

Pour into an elegant cup or glass, and admire! Then drink . . .

1615 Anne of Austria, daughter of Philip III of Spain, marries the infant Louis XIII of France and takes him Spanish chocolate as a gift. She is accompanied by a maid whose sole purpose is to make her chocolate every day. Chocolate soon becomes fashionable in the French court.

Chocolate **connoisseurs** believe that the best chocolates contain a blend of four or more different beans, each from a different country: Venezuela, Brazil, Madagascar and the Ivory Coast.

1660 Chocolate is first recorded as being for sale in England; the beverage is available in Oxford.

Chocolate

Chocolate is . . .

velvety
dark
rewarding
delicate
exciting

How chocolate is made

Pods from the cacao tree are **harvested** twice a year. The beans are gathered and then dried for 24–48 hours, after which time the bean is split and its pulp removed. The pulp and beans are then placed in mounds on banana leaves and covered.

The pulp ferments while covered by banana leaves and the beans absorb the byproducts of this process. The beans are left to dry in the **sun** after the fermentation has finished.

Chocolate manufacturers buy the fermented cocoa beans and clean them. The beans are then roasted. A process called **winnowing** separates the hard shell from the centre of the bean, called the nib.

Chocolate

The nib is ground down and becomes chocolate (or cocoa) **liquor**, which is the main ingredient in chocolate.

The chocolate liquor is **melted**. To make the product more delicate, extra cocoa butter is added (the liquor naturally contains approximately 45% cocoa butter). Sugar and vanilla – and dry milk powder for milk chocolate – are also added.

The chocolate mass is then subjected to a process called conching. The mixture is placed in a folding or wave motion by a conching machine for several hours, and sometimes days, in order to reduce the size of all the particles in the mixture. This process results in an **exceptionally smooth texture**.

The conched mixture is allowed to cool to about 32°C (90°F) while it is still moving in the machine. This is said to 'temper' the product. Once this is completed, the chocolate is made into bars. **Yum!**

1696 The mayor of Zurich visits Belgium
and takes chocolate back to
Switzerland with him.

Chocolate

'Nine out of ten people like chocolate . . .

'The tenth person always lies.'

John G. Tullius, American artist and cartoonist

Sir Hans Sloane (1660–1753), the physician of Queen Anne of England, was reportedly the first person to mix chocolate successfully with milk. The resulting drink was used for **restorative purposes**.

Chocolate

A **milk chocolate drink** was first marketed
in England in the early eighteenth century.
A later advertisement for the product by the
Fry company emphasised the medicinal
value of the drink, 'its lightness on the
stomach and its great use in all
consumptive cases'.

Chocolate bars were made possible by the invention of the cocoa press in the eighteenth century. By the middle of the nineteenth century, both Fry and Son and the Cadbury company were selling 'tablets' (blocks) of chocolate to the English public.

1728 Walter Churchman manufactures chocolate in Bristol; he is the first chocolate maker in England. He is granted letters patent by King George II in 1729.

Chocolate

'The average Englishman starts his day with a walk in the park, afterwards he saunters to some coffee or chocolate house frequented by the persons he would see, for it is a sort of rule with the English to go once a day at least to houses of this sort . . .'

Lewes, Baron de Pollnitz, writing in 1745

Chocolate . . .

Makes the world go round!

Chocolate-lovers are in good company.
Napoleon carried chocolate with him on
military escapades, eating it when he needed
energy quickly.

1761 The Fry family buys Walter Churchman's business, making them the oldest chocolate manufacturers in Great Britain.

'The ladies of the New World, it seems, are mad for chocolate. We are told that, not content to drink it every moment of the day at home, they sometimes have it brought to them in church . . .

Chocolate

'This habit brought down on them the censure of their confessors, who ended up, however, taking their part and sharing their chocolate.'

Alexandre Dumas, *fils*, (1824–1895),
French writer

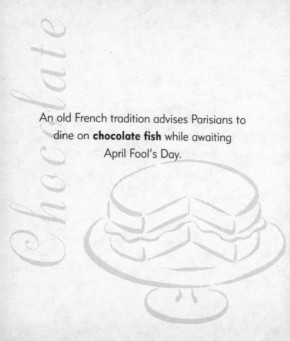

An old French tradition advises Parisians to dine on **chocolate fish** while awaiting April Fool's Day.

Chocolate

1766 Lombard of France, purportedly the oldest chocolaterie in that country, opens for business.

Chocolate is . . .

smooth
tempting
tantalising
mouth-watering
delicious

Chocolate

'There is a tendency, also, to associate very dark
foods, such as coffee, chocolate, truffles, caviar,
and cèpes, as well as plum cake, with excitement
and luxury. We feel obscurely that such strange
dark stuff must be meaningful and ancient.'

Margaret Visser, Canadian writer

Chocolate, Date and Almond Torte

250 g whole almonds (unpeeled)

250 g dark chocolate

6 egg whites

½ cup castor sugar

250 g dates

(pitted and chopped into small pieces)

Place almonds and chocolate in a blender and chop into chunky pieces. Cut dates finely. Beat egg whites until they form stiff peaks and gradually add castor sugar. Fold in almonds, dates and chocolate and combine. Pour into a greased, lined tin. Bake at 180°C for 45 minutes or until cooked. Cool and turn out onto a wire cake rack. Refrigerate overnight. Dust with icing sugar and serve with fruits in season.

1828 The Dutchman Coenraad van Houten develops what we now know as cocoa by removing a large amount of the cocoa butter from cocoa to make a dry powder.

Chocolate

Most of us associate chocolate with
romance, with good reason. When chocolate
first became popular in Europe several
centuries ago it was thought to invigorate
men and make women less inhibited, thus
making it the ideal gift to bestow upon
your sweetheart.

'Chocolate is heavenly, mellow, sensual, deep. Dark, sumptuous, gratifying, potent, dense, creamy, seductive, suggestive, rich, excessive, silky, smooth, luxurious, celestial . . .

'Chocolate is downfall, happiness, pleasure, love, ecstasy, fantasy . . . chocolate makes us wicked, guilty, sinful, healthy, chic, happy.'

Elaine Sherman, American writer

1842 Cadbury's chocolate company creates the first chocolate bar, made possible by the invention of the cocoa press in the eighteenth century.

Chocolate

Chocolate tastes good with . . .

raisins

caramel

coffee

coconut

marzipan

Brownies

2 eggs

½ cup melted butter (or margarine)

¾ cup sugar

⅔ cup plain flour (unsifted)

1 tsp vanilla

¼ tsp baking powder

¾ cup drinking chocolate

¼ tsp salt

½ cup chopped nuts of your choice
(optional)

Preheat oven to 180°C (350°F). Beat eggs with sugar and vanilla. Add melted butter; mix ingredients together. Sift the drinking chocolate with the plain flour, baking powder and salt. Gradually beat these ingredients into the egg mixture. Add nuts if desired. Spread onto a greased 8-inch pan and bake for 20 minutes. Once cooled, cut into squares and serve.

1875 Daniel Peters, a Swiss chocolate maker, mixes Henri Nestlé's condensed milk with chocolate, and the two men produce the first milk chocolate.

Chocolate

Milk chocolate is the most popular type of chocolate. It is made up of approximately 50% sugar, 35% milk solids and 15% cocoa solids.

Dark chocolate comprises 5–10% of the total chocolate consumption in most countries around the world. Its composition is usually about 55% sugar and 45% cocoa solids. Sometimes it will contain small amounts of salt and lecithin.

Is **white chocolate** really chocolate? Some say that, as it contains no chocolate liquor (it's made from sugar, cocoa butter or vegetable fat, dry milk solids and flavouring), it can't truly be called chocolate. Others, however, maintain that it merits the name 'chocolate' because of the presence of cocoa butter.

1894 Milton Hershey invents the Hershey Bar by experimenting with milk chocolate.

Chocolate

Chocolate does **melt in your mouth** – literally! Dark chocolate starts to melt at 34–35°C (93°F), which is just below body temperature. Milk chocolate melts at slightly lower temperatures.

Chocolate

When in doubt . . .

Apply chocolate!

'Chocolate, of course, is the stuff of which fantasies are made. Rich, dark, velvety-smooth fantasies that envelop the senses and stir the passions. Chocolate is madness; chocolate is delight.'

Judith Olney, American chef

Chocolate contains phenylethylamine, or PEA. PEA is a chemical also found in the brain and is responsible for raising blood pressure and increasing heart rate; it is released when feelings of **lust or passion** are present. No wonder chocolate makes you feel like you're in love!

Chocolate

There are approximately 5 to 10 mg of **caffeine** in 30 g (1 oz) of bittersweet chocolate, but there are 100 to 150 mg in a 250 ml (8 oz) cup of brewed coffee.

Chocolate-covered Strawberries

12 large, ripe strawberries with stems still on
270 g semisweet or dark chocolate

Melt the chocolate in a double boiler over hot, but not boiling, water. Remove from heat when there are no more lumps in the chocolate. Dip the strawberries one at a time into the chocolate. Lay the strawberries carefully on a nonstick surface such as waxed paper, and then refrigerate until the chocolate sets. Eat within 24 hours.

Chocolate is . . .

sexy
vital
sinful
addictive
naughty

Chocolate

On 29 June 1995, chocolate was one of the gifts exchanged between Russian cosmonauts and American **astronauts** aboard the Russian space station Mir.

Chocolate

'Life without chocolate . . .

'is life lacking something important.'

Marcia Colman and Frederic Morton, American writers

The **chocolate chip biscuit** was discovered by accident. In 1933, while American Ruth Wakefield was hastily preparing a batch of chocolate biscuits, she neglected to melt the chocolate first and instead used whole lumps of chocolate, thinking they would melt during baking . . .

Chocolate

However, the lumps of chocolate stayed lumpy. No one complained about the results, and the chocolate chip cookie was born.

'Most chocolate chip cookies do not have enough
chocolate chips in them.'

Judith Olney, American writer

'My desire for chocolate has seldom abated, even in times of great peril.'

Marcel Desaulniers, American chef and creator of the 'Death by Chocolate' dessert

1897 Cadbury begins to manufacture milk chocolate in competition with the Swiss.

Chocolate

The white film that can sometimes be found on chocolate is called **bloom**, and it occurs when chocolate has been exposed to heat. The heat causes some of the fat in the chocolate to melt and rise to the surface. It then sets as a white film when the chocolate cools. Bloom does not spoil chocolate.

The flavour of milk chocolate starts to deteriorate after about six months. **The flavour of dark chocolate**, like that of fine wine, improves with time for up to 18 to 24 months.

'It has been shown as proof positive that carefully prepared chocolate is as healthful a food as it is pleasant; that it is nourishing and easily digested . . . that it is above all helpful to people who must do a great deal of mental work.'

Anthelme Brillat-Savarin (1755–1826),
French magistrate and gastronome

The best temperature for storing chocolate is around 10°C (50°F), so to make your chocolate **last longer,** keep it in the refrigerator. But wrap it well: chocolate is a fat-based substance and will pick up any odours.

Chocolate

Chocolate-lovers have long believed in the **health-giving effects** of chocolate, and now the experts agree: chocolate contains high levels of phenol, a chemical that can help reduce the risk of heart disease.

'Chocolate is not only pleasant of taste, but it is also a veritable balm of the mouth, for the maintaining of all glands and humours in a good state of health. Thus it is, that all who drink it, possess a sweet breath.'

Stephani Blancardi (1650–1702),
Italian physician

Great news for **chocoholics** . . . Chocolate can actually *prevent* tooth cavities. While the sugar contained in chocolate is a major contributing cause of tooth decay, chocolate itself is made up of elements that obstruct the formation of plaque. So chocolate effectively neutralises any cavity-causing potential in the sugar!

1905 Cadbury's Dairy Milk Bar is introduced.

Chocolate

Chocolate contains easily digested
carbohydrates and is a high-energy food.
It's often recommended for bushwalkers and
high-performance sportsmen and women –
and, of course, for anyone else who
needs a boost.

'Good chocolate won't make you sick. It won't even make you fat. Look at me, and I eat it all day long.'

Robert Linxie, French chocolatier

Chocolate tastes good with . . .

vanilla

milk

strawberries

ice-cream

CHOCOLATE!

For a wintertime taste sensation . . .

Try some raspberry or peppermint schnapps
in hot chocolate

Chocolate

1908 Toblerone is invented by the Swiss Theodor Tobler. Each piece of the new chocolate bar is made in the triangular shape of an Alpine peak.

Chocolate

Diamonds aren't a girl's best friend . . .

Chocolate is!

Chocolate is . . .

faithful
sweet
silky-smooth
irresistible
unforgettable

Chocolate movie trivia: The 'blood' draining out of the shower in the famous shower scene of Alfred Hitchcock's film *Psycho* was actually chocolate syrup.

Chocolate

1920 Cadbury's Flake is introduced.

Chocolate crackles

250 g copha
1 cup coconut
1 cup icing sugar (sifted)
3 tbsp cocoa
4 cups puffed rice cereal

Combine all ingredients except copha in a mixing bowl. Heat copha and pour over mixture; combine well. Spoon the mixture into paper patty cases and refrigerate.

'Does the notion of chocolate preclude the concept of free will?'

Sandra Boynton, American cartoonist

Chocolate

Three billion pounds (nearly 1.5 billion kilograms) of chocolate are consumed **worldwide** each year.

Chocolate sauce

100 g butter
100 g semisweet chocolate
325 g caster sugar
350 g evaporated milk
a pinch of salt
5 ml vanilla extract

Melt butter and chocolate together in a saucepan. Add sugar, milk and salt and cook for 20 to 25 minutes over moderate heat; this should allow the mixture to thicken. Add vanilla and stir into mixture. (This sauce will harden when refrigerated, so reheat it in a saucepan to melt.)

Chocolate sauce can be poured over ice-cream, cakes and anything else you can think of . . .

The retail chocolate industry of the USA is worth approximately **$13 billion** a year.

Chocolate

'It flatters you for a while; it warms you for an
instant; then, all of a sudden, it kindles
a mortal fever in you.'

Madame de Sévigné (1620–1705),
French courtesan and writer

The average annual per capita **consumption** of chocolate in the UK is nearly 30 lb (9.3 kg), which would cost the average Briton about £1.18 a week! But this figure is beaten by the Swiss at 10 kg and Australians at 10.5 kg. It's a good thing chocolate's a health food . . .

1923 H. B. Reese, a former employee of Hershey's, begins making Reese's Peanut Butter Cups.

'Persons who drink chocolate regularly are conspicuous for unfailing health and immunity from the host of minor ailments which mar the enjoyment of life; they are also less inclined to lose weight . . .'

Anthelme Brillat-Savarin (1755–1826),
French magistrate and gastronome

Chocolate

About 15% of all chocolate purchases are made at **Christmas** time, although this can vary from country to country. Australians buy more chocolate at Easter than at Christmas.

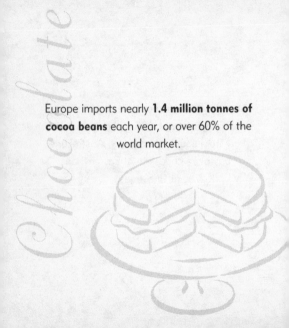

Europe imports nearly **1.4 million tonnes of cocoa beans** each year, or over 60% of the world market.

O chocolate, chocolate!
wherefore art thou chocolate?

'Other things are just food.
But chocolate's chocolate.'

Patrick Skene Catling, American writer

Chocolate

1930 Franklin Mars invents the Snickers bar.
Fry's invents the Crunchie.

Chocolate

'What use are cartridges in battle?

'I always carry chocolate instead.'

George Bernard Shaw (1856–1950),
Irish playwright, from **Arms and the Man**

Chocolate is . . .

mesmerising

warm

silky

comforting

bittersweet

Chocolate

1932 The Mars Bar is developed and sold.

'It's not that chocolates are a substitute
for love . . .

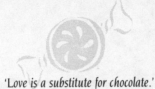

'*Love is a substitute for chocolate.*'

Miranda Ingram

The French government strictly legislates the production of chocolate. To be called 'chocolate' in France the confectionery must contain no animal or vegetable fats; only cocoa butter is authorised. As well as this, **French chocolates** must contain at least 43% cocoa liquor and 26% pure cocoa liquor.

Chocolate

More wintertime taste sensations . . .

Add some amaretto and/or rum, or rum and
Kahlua to hot chocolate

Chocolate

Chocolate tastes good with . . .

figs

honey

cream

rum

sugar

Chocolate stimulates the release of endorphins in the body. Endorphins generate feelings of **euphoria** and block pain and are usually produced during strenuous physical exercise.

West Africa produces most of the cocoa beans consumed throughout the world – about 60%, in fact. Beans are also produced in Central and South America – where Brazil is the major supplier – and the Caribbean islands.

Chocolate

Chocolate is . . .

essential

rich

sensuous

delectable

creamy

Chocolate

1934 Caramello appears in shops.

Chocolates are dipped in **couverture chocolate** to give them the glossy finish we see on many chocolate confectioneries. Couverture chocolate is different to other chocolate because it contains no fat other than its own natural cocoa butter.

Easy chocolate mousse

170 g dark chocolate chips
¼ cup boiling water
1 egg
1 tsp vanilla extract
1 cup cream

Chocolate

Place chocolate chips and boiling water in blender on high speed for 15 seconds. Then add the rest of the ingredients and blend until all the ingredients have combined. Pour the mixture into glasses and chill until firm.

Bakers' chocolate is couverture chocolate with vegetable fat added and a higher sugar content. It doesn't have the same rich flavour as couverture but is easier to use because its higher fat content means that it doesn't require the 'tempering' needed for couverture.

1935 The Aero bar makes its first appearance.

Bitter chocolate would test the devotion of any chocoholic – it contains about 50% cocoa solids and no sugar at all. This unsweetened substance is used mainly in baking and confectionery, as it gives a very strong chocolate flavour.

Chocolate

Real chocoholics would probably never eat **carob**, but many people enjoy the taste of this 'chocolate alternative'. Carob is made from the beans of the carob tree, a native of Mediterranean countries and the Middle East.

Yet more wintertime taste sensations . . .

Try hot chocolate with a dash each of peppermint schnapps, Kahlua and dark creme de cacao.

1936 Maltesers and Quality Street are introduced.

A scene from James Barrie's famous play **Peter Pan** has its origins in a real little boy's devotion to his chocolate.

Sylvia Llewelyn-Davies warned her young son not to eat any more chocolates or he would make himself sick tomorrow . . .

Chocolate

The child answered, 'I shall be sick tonight', and then deliberately ate more chocolate.

Barrie included this exchange in **Peter Pan** and paid the young Llewelyn-Davies a copyright fee of one ha'penny per performance.

Some chocolates are better for us than others. The more expensive dark chocolates are usually lower in sugar and fat than their less costly counterparts. As they are usually **richer in flavour**, too, you might be inclined to eat less of them.

'If I were a headmaster, I would get rid of the history teacher and get a chocolate teacher instead and my pupils would study a subject that affected all of them.'

Roald Dahl, British writer

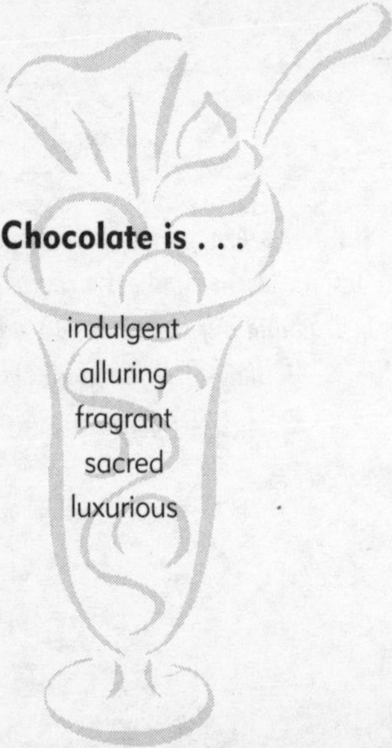

Chocolate is . . .

indulgent

alluring

fragrant

sacred

luxurious

Chocolate

In its pure, unsweetened form, chocolate is used in several **savoury dishes**. The most famous is probably *mole poblano*, a Mexican speciality of turkey cooked in a chocolate, chilli and nut sauce.

The **cocoa bean** contains caffeine, theobromine, calcium, phosphorus, potassium, iron, sodium, carbohydrate, protein, fat, starch, thiamine, vitamin A and riboflavin but not, unfortunately, in enough quantities to make it wholly nutritionally sound.

1937 Kit Kat, Rolo and Smarties are all invented in this year.

Chocolate tastes good with . . .

oranges
macadamias
pistachios
chestnuts

Chocolate

If you want to enjoy the aroma of chocolate all day long, you'll love the '**chocolate plant**'. *Cosmos atrosanguineus*, or Chocolate Cosmos, has a slightly spiced chocolate aroma that deepens at dusk. This unique plant originates from Mexico, the traditional 'birthplace' of chocolate.

Easter eggs

To make your own Easter eggs or rabbits
you will need an egg or rabbit mould and, of
course, some chocolate. Break the chocolate
into pieces and melt it in a double saucepan
over boiling water. Once melted, pour the
chocolate into the mould and tip the mould
from side to side until it is fully coated.
Then . . .

Leave the moulds to cool on nonstick paper with the hollow side down (but do not refrigerate). For an Easter egg, mould two halves and join them together by heating a baking sheet and quickly touching the edge of each half against the hot metal. This will cause the chocolate to begin to melt; the two halves will seal when joined together.

1940 The Mars company invents M&Ms for soldiers going to World War II.

Chocolate

Many people believe that chocolate and **cocaine** come from the same plant. This is entirely false. Chocolate comes from the *cacao* tree; cocaine comes from the *coca* shrub.

Frogs in the pond

Make one bowl of green jelly and decorate
creatively with chocolate frogs (and any
other chocolate confectionery you desire).

Chocolate is . . .

sticky
sublime
aromatic
fulfilling
enticing

If chocolate be the food
of love, play on:

Give me excess of it . . .